D1499416

New Albany - Floyd County Public Library
3 3110 00437 2551

Connections!

BUILDINGS

CAROLINE GRIMSHAW

TEXT **IQBAL HUSSAIN**

CONSULTANT **ZIONA STRELITZ**
ANTHROPOLOGIST/PLANNER
SPECIALIST IN PEOPLE'S USE OF THE BUILT ENVIRONMENT

ILLUSTRATIONS **NICK DUFFY** ☆ **SPIKE GERRELL** ☆ **JO MOORE**

A TWO-CAN BOOK
PUBLISHED BY
THOMSON LEARNING
NEW YORK

Connections!

BUILDINGS

CREATIVE AND EDITORIAL DIRECTOR
CONCEPT/FORMAT/DESIGN
CAROLINE GRIMSHAW

TEXT IQBAL HUSSAIN
CONSULTANT ZIONA STRELITZ
ANTHROPOLOGIST/PLANNER
SPECIALIST IN PEOPLE'S USE OF
THE BUILT ENVIRONMENT

ILLUSTRATIONS
NICK DUFFY ☆ SPIKE GERRELL ☆ JO MOORE

THANKS TO
DEBBIE DORMAN PICTURE RESEARCH
JUSTINE COOPER AND ROBERT SVED EDITORIAL SUPPORT
AND ANDREW JARVIS ☆ RUTH KING
CHARLES SHAAR MURRAY

BOOKS IN THIS SERIES

PEOPLE
BUILDINGS
EARTH

PUBLISHED IN 1995 BY TWO-CAN PUBLISHING LTD
IN ASSOCIATION WITH THOMSON LEARNING, NEW YORK.

PRINTED AND BOUND IN BELGIUM BY PROOST NV

LIBRARY OF CONGRESS CATALOGING-IN-PUBLICATION DATA
GRIMSHAW, CAROLINE.
BUILDINGS / CAROLINE GRIMSHAW [CREATIVE AND EDITORIAL DIRECTOR] : TEXT. IQBAL HUSSAIN : ILLUSTRATIONS, NICK DUFFY, SPIKE GERRELL, JO MOORE.
P. CM. — (CONNECTIONS!) INCLUDES INDEX.
ISBN 1-56847-452-0
1. BUILDINGS--MISCELLANEA--JUVENILE LITERATURE. 2. ARCHITECTURE – MISCELLANEA — JUVENILE LITERATURE. [1. BUILDINGS. 2. ARCHITECTURE.] I. HUSSAIN, IQBAL, 1971- . II. DUFFY, NICK, ILL. III. GERRELL, SPIKE, ILL. IV. MOORE, JO, ILL. V. TITLE. VI. SERIES: CONNECTIONS! (THOMSON LEARNING : FIRM)
TH149.G75 1995
721--DC20 95-6699

Contents

DISCOVER THE CONNECTIONS THROUGH QUESTIONS AND ANSWERS...

YOU CAN READ THIS BOOK FROM START TO FINISH OR LEAPFROG THROUGH THE SECTIONS FOLLOWING THE PATHS SUGGESTED IN THESE SPECIAL "CONNECT! BOXES".

Connect!

ENJOY YOUR JOURNEY OF DISCOVERY AND UNDERSTANDING.

Connections!

It's time to ask yourself,

just what is a building?

Where is the world's tallest building?

How do walls hold up roofs?

Are buildings always made of brick and stone?

You'll find all these questions (and more!) answered in PART ONE of your journey of discovery and understanding. Turn the page!

QUESTION

1 What is a building?

What do a house, an office, and a mosque have in common? They're all buildings, that's what!

A BUILDING IS ANY MAN-MADE STRUCTURE WHICH ENCLOSES SOME OF THE SPACE AROUND IT AND WHICH PROVIDES PROTECTION FROM THE ELEMENTS.

Connect!

WHY DON'T ALL BUILDINGS LOOK THE SAME? YOU'LL FIND OUT IN PART 2.

Look at these pictures. Which are buildings?

1 THE SYDNEY OPERA HOUSE

2 THE EIFFEL TOWER

3 THE PYRAMIDS

4 STONEHENGE

THE ANSWERS ARE HIDDEN ON THIS PAGE.

QUESTION

2 Why did people start to make buildings?

Connect!

LATER, BUILDINGS BECAME MORE THAN JUST A WAY OF COPING WITH THE ELEMENTS. CHECK OUT Q26.

It was the need for survival.

About 2.5 million years ago, early humans lived in caves. The caves provided them with shelter and also protected them from wild animals.

A cave painting of a bull in Lascaux, France.

Connect!

DOES THE CLIMATE STILL PLAY A PART IN HOW A BUILDING LOOKS? FIND OUT IN Q25.

But what happened when there were no caves? Humans had to learn to make their own homes. The ability to build freestanding shelters gave people more freedom to move in search of food and favorable conditions.

BUILDINGS GAVE THEM:

- PROTECTION FROM THE SUN.
- A ROOF OVER THEIR HEADS.
- SOMEWHERE TO PUT THEIR BELONGINGS.
- A PLACE TO STAY WARM AND DRY.

Early buildings were made from easily found materials such as wood, reeds, and animal skins. Some huts were built from a mixture of branches and mammoth bones.

THE ANSWERS TO QUESTION 1 ARE: 1, 2, AND 3 ARE BUILDINGS; 4 IS NOT.

QUESTION

Are any really early buildings still standing today?

Little evidence remains of early buildings.

This is because they were built from materials that would have broken down or been blown away a long time ago. But, in 1965, 21 huts were discovered in Nice, France. They are about 400,000 years old, which makes them the world's oldest known buildings. The huts were found close to each other, so the people must have lived as part of a community. This settlement is one of the earliest examples of people living together in this way.

QUESTION

Who were the first architects?

Architects are people who design buildings.

The earliest architects were humans escaping from their caves. But the Middle East regions of Mesopotamia and Egypt had the first examples of formal architecture, around 5,000 years ago.

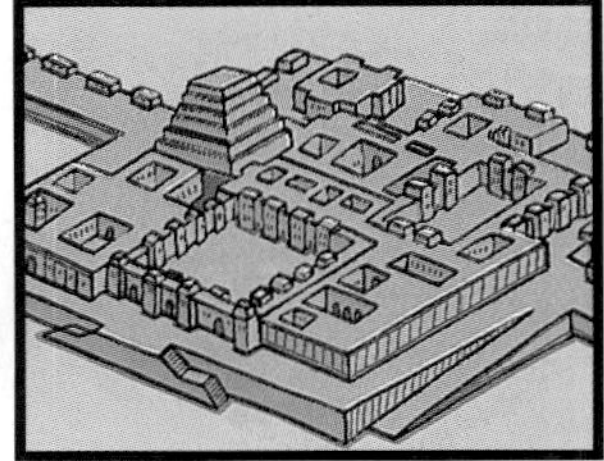

THE CITADEL OF KING SARGON II WAS BUILT IN KHORSABAD, ASSYRIA. IT HAD MANY TEMPLES, PALACES, HOUSES, AND A TALL PYRAMIDLIKE STRUCTURE CALLED A ZIGGURAT.

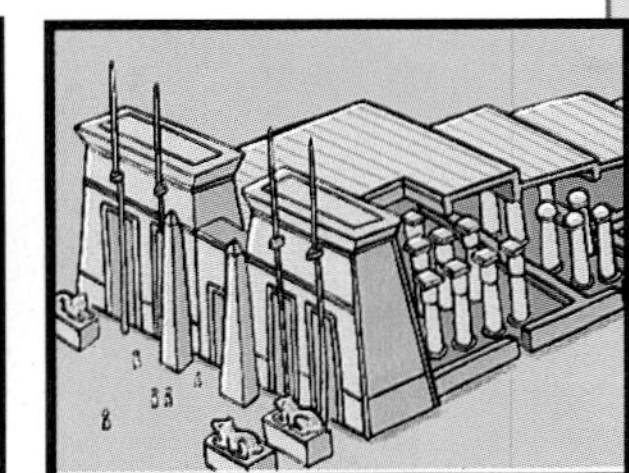

THE TEMPLE AT KARNAK, EGYPT, WAS DEDICATED TO THE MOON GOD KHONS. THE ENTRANCE WAS GUARDED BY TWO LARGE TOWERS CALLED PYLONS. COLUMNS HELD UP THE TEMPLE ROOF.

WHAT SHOULD BE ON AN ARCHITECT'S CHECKLIST?

- ✔ **FUNCTION** EVERY BUILDING NEEDS TO BE DESIGNED FOR THE RIGHT PURPOSE.
- ✔ **APPEARANCE** THE LOOK OF THE BUILDING SHOULD RELATE TO ITS FUNCTION, THE CHOICE OF MATERIALS, AND THE CLIMATE.
- ✔ **DURABILITY** THE BUILDING MUST BE ABLE TO SURVIVE THE EFFECTS OF THE WEATHER AND BE EASY TO REPAIR.

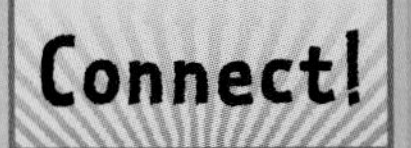

Connect!

SOME ARCHITECTS HAVE BECOME VERY FAMOUS. SEE Q29.

QUESTION

5 What are the smallest, tallest

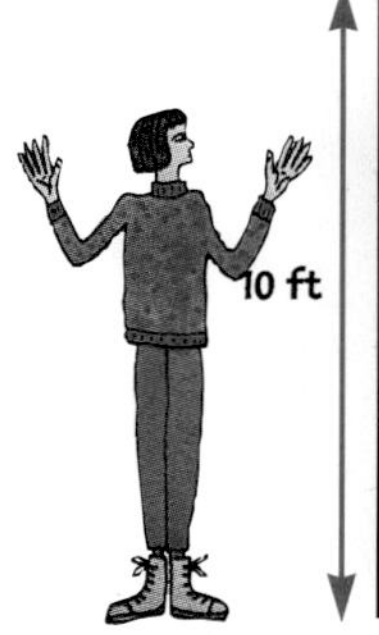

10 ft

6 ft

THIS IS SMALL

A 19th-century fisherman's cottage in Conwy, North Wales, has just two tiny rooms and a staircase. It is only 6 ft wide and 10 ft high.

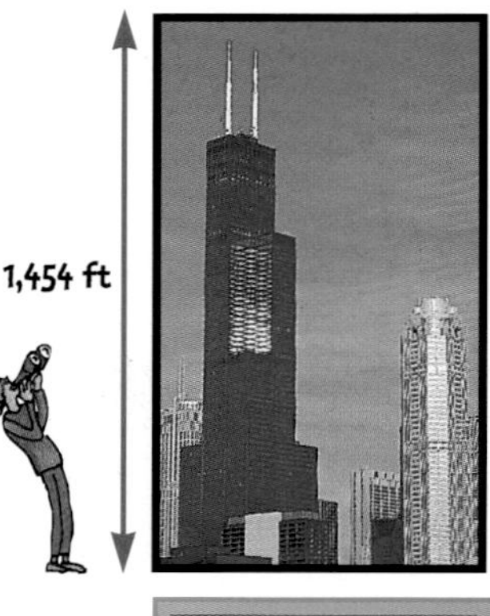

1,454 ft

THIS IS TALL

The Sears Tower in Chicago, rises to 1,454 ft. It has 110 stories, 104 elevators, 18 escalators, and 16,100 windows.

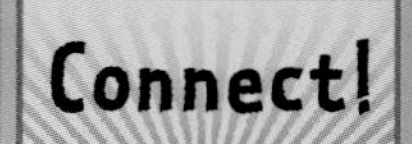

Connect! TURN TO Q28 TO FIND OUT WHY SKYSCRAPERS DON'T FALL DOWN.

QUESTION

6 Are all buildings built from the

No. Some buildings start at ground level and then work their way down. Others are raised above the ground.

1 Buildings with basements

The basement is the lowest floor of a building. It is usually found completely below ground level.

During the bombings of World War II (1939–45), people sheltered in basements and cellars for protection.

2 Going down

There is a strong tradition of people living underground in parts of Europe, Australia, the Middle East, and China.

In Coober Pedy, north of Adelaide, Australia, people escape the unbearable summer heat by constructing homes underground.

LIVING UNDERGROUND

IS GOOD BECAUSE...

- STABLE TEMPERATURES AND HUMIDITY CAN MEAN PEOPLE LIVING BELOW GROUND HAVE SMOOTHER SKIN AND SUFFER LESS FROM RHEUMATISM.
- THE AIR IS FREE FROM POLLUTION, MAKING UNDERGROUND DWELLINGS PARTICULARLY GOOD FOR ASTHMA SUFFERERS.
- BUILDING UNDERGROUND REDUCES PRESSURE ON SURFACE LAND.

IS BAD BECAUSE...

- THERE MAY NOT BE ENOUGH NATURAL LIGHT. RELYING ON ARTIFICIAL LIGHT CAN MAKE YOU SLEEPY AND DEPRESSED.
- UNLESS SUBTERRANEAN COMMUNITIES ARE DEVELOPED, YOU MAY START TO FEEL LONELY AND ISOLATED.

☆ IN THE 10TH AND 11TH CENTURIES, ENORMOUS **UNDERGROUND CITIES** WERE BUILT IN THE CAPPADOCIA REGION OF TURKEY. THOUSANDS OF CHRISTIANS LIVED THERE TO AVOID ISLAMIC INVADERS.

nd narrowest buildings?

13 ft

THIS IS NARROW

So many people liked the view of the canals in Amsterdam, Holland, that houses were constructed as narrow as possible. This way more buildings with a view of the water could be fitted in.

178 acres

AND THIS IS LARGE!

The Imperial Palace in Beijing, China, which is made up of five halls and 17 smaller palaces, covers an area of 178 acres.

☆ **WHAT IS THE STRANGEST BUILDING?** THAT'S A MATTER OF TASTE! YOU MUST DECIDE FOR YOURSELF WHEN YOU'VE FINISHED READING THIS BOOK.

ground up?

Connect!

SOME BUILDINGS LOOK SO ODD THAT IT IS HARD TO IMAGINE THEY COULD BE USED AS BUILDINGS. CHECK THEM OUT IN Q23.

3 Buildings raised above the ground

In India and Indonesia – countries that experience heavy rainfall – houses are sometimes built on stilts. When the land floods, the buildings stay dry. The space under the stilts also provides room to keep any pets and other animals.

In this Indonesian house, a ladder made from thick branches rises up to the front door.

Stilt buildings are not as common in Western countries. But the architect Charles Edouard Jenneret (1887–1966), who was known as Le Corbusier, tried to change this. It had long been his wish to free or liberate buildings from their ground-level sites. With the invention of reinforced concrete, he was able to realize his dreams. He designed several buildings that were supported by stilts, or pilotis.

SWISS HOUSE, CITE UNIVERSITAIRE (PARIS, FRANCE). This university building made Le Corbusier famous. It literally stood out from the other traditional campus buildings.

DOUBLE HOUSE (STUTTGART, GERMANY). This large concrete house is perched on several pilotis, leaving a gap underneath.

WHY DO YOU THINK LE CORBUSIER LEFT THIS GAP?

Connect!

HOW ARE BUILDINGS ADAPTED TO COPE WITH LITTLE RAIN OR INTENSE HEAT? TURN TO Q25.

Connect!

THE VISIONS AND IDEAS OF ARCHITECTS HAVE SHAPED THE WAY OUR WORLD LOOKS. TURN TO Q29 AND Q34 TO SEE IF THIS HAS ALWAYS BEEN SUCCESSFUL.

Why don't all roofs look the same?

A roof is a covering over the top of a building. It protects the interior from the elements. It can also stop heat escaping or help to ventilate the building.

A ROOF HAS TWO MAIN PARTS:

1 THE COVERING 2 THE SUPPORTING FRAME

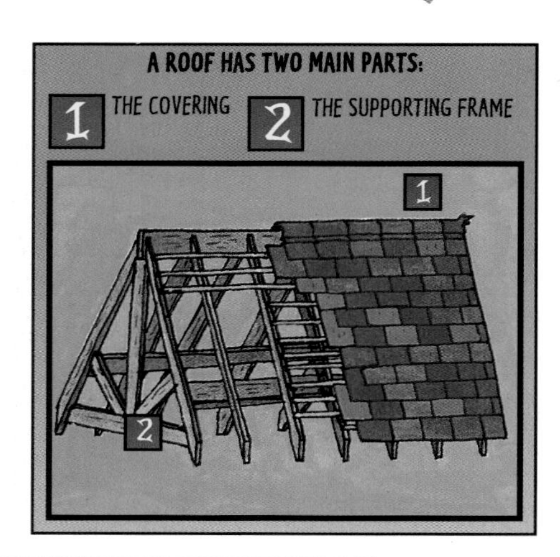

Domes

A dome is a convex roof. This means its surface is curved like half a ball. The weight at the top helps the dome keep its shape. Domes can be built in all shapes and sizes.

JUST AS A BUILDING STYLE IS DETERMINED BY VARIOUS FACTORS, SO IS THE LOOK OF A ROOF. FOR EXAMPLE:
THE LOCAL TRADITION; THE CLIMATE; THE MATERIALS AVAILABLE; THE COST INVOLVED; THE SKILL OF THE BUILDER AND ARCHITECT; THE FASHION OF THE TIME.

The Dome of the Rock mosque, Jerusalem, Israel, has a hemispherical dome.

The mosque at Santa Sophia, Istanbul, Turkey, has a saucer dome.

Different roof styles have different names...

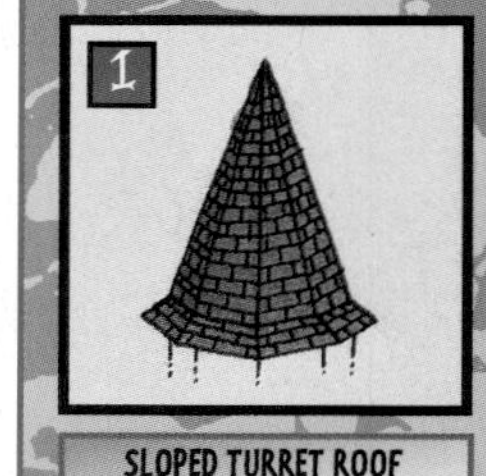

1 SLOPED TURRET ROOF

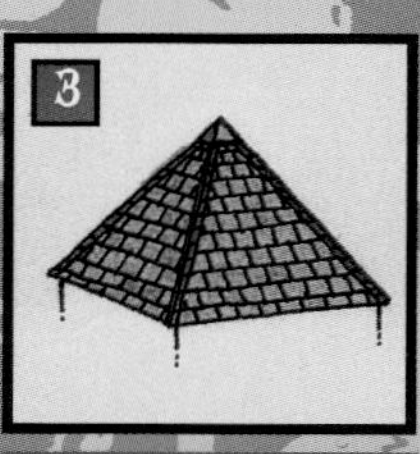

2 HIP ROOF

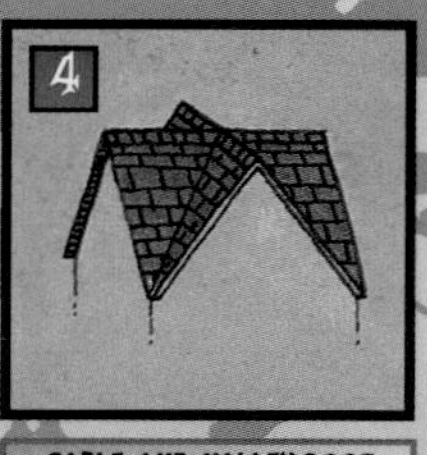

3 PAVILION ROOF

4 GABLE-AND-VALLEY ROOF

IT'S A COVER-UP!

Many roofs are covered with clay tiles or slate. Asphalt is used to waterproof flat roofs. Some buildings have thatched roofs. These are made from thick layers of straw or reed.

To stop grain from getting damp, the Dogon people in Mali, West Africa, store it in thatched huts built on wooden platforms.

St. Basil's Cathedral, Russia, has eight onion domes, all with different designs on them.

TURN TO Q25 TO FIND OUT WHY SOME ROOFS TURN BRIGHT GREEN.

Question 8 What holds up the roof?

Walls. A wall is a continuous structure that surrounds or divides up a building.

1 WALL BUILDINGS

In this type of building, the walls are completely solid. They play a major part in holding the building together. Being solid, the walls can comfortably bear the whole weight of the roof.

2 FRAME BUILDINGS

The building is held together by an arrangement of posts. This frame of horizontal and vertical beams is strong enough to support the roof. Other walls and partitions may be added. These walls do not hold up the roof, but divide up the building.

In the Mediterranean, mud-brick houses have solid rectangular walls to hold up the flat roof.

A British timber-framed house is a good example of a frame building.

Connect!

WHY DO STONE WALLS ALL LOOK DIFFERENT? CHECK OUT Q15.

Question 9 Are ceilings and floors the same thing?

No. In most modern buildings, there is a gap between one floor and another.

This gap is used to hide all the cables, electrical wiring, and water pipes. But, in the past, the floor of one room was just the ceiling of the room below. In Britain, by the 16th century, the exposed timbers were covered with boards and stucco – a kind of plaster. Elaborately decorated stucco ceilings became popular in the 17th century.

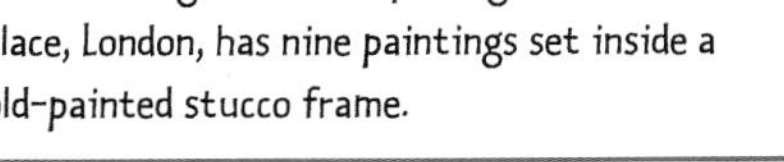

The ceiling of the Banqueting House, Whitehall Palace, London, has nine paintings set inside a gold-painted stucco frame.

Why do buildings have windows?

Windows are our link with the outside world. They let light into a room and open up to let in fresh air.

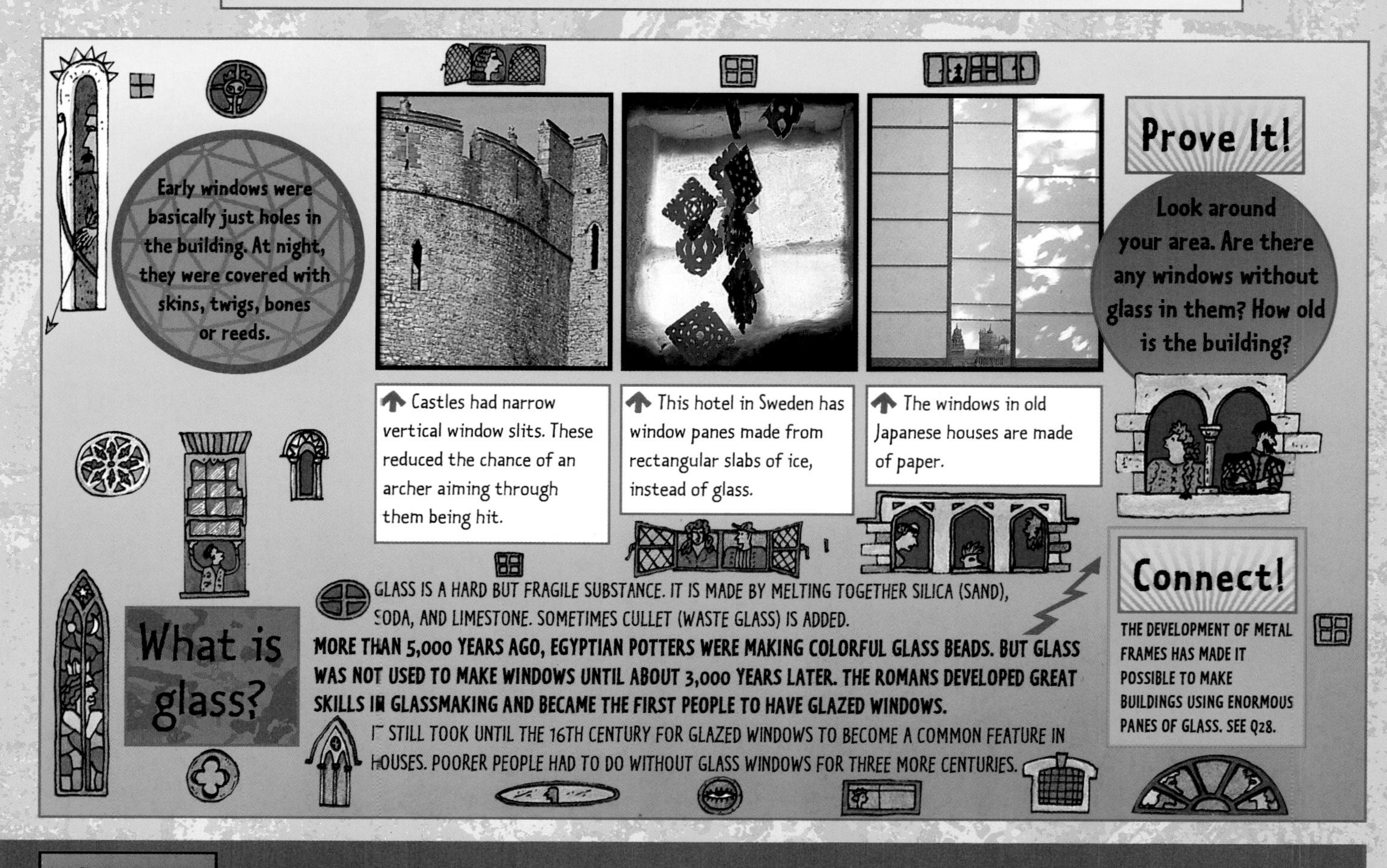

Early windows were basically just holes in the building. At night, they were covered with skins, twigs, bones or reeds.

↑ Castles had narrow vertical window slits. These reduced the chance of an archer aiming through them being hit.

↑ This hotel in Sweden has window panes made from rectangular slabs of ice, instead of glass.

↑ The windows in old Japanese houses are made of paper.

Prove It!

Look around your area. Are there any windows without glass in them? How old is the building?

What is glass?

GLASS IS A HARD BUT FRAGILE SUBSTANCE. IT IS MADE BY MELTING TOGETHER SILICA (SAND), SODA, AND LIMESTONE. SOMETIMES CULLET (WASTE GLASS) IS ADDED.

MORE THAN 5,000 YEARS AGO, EGYPTIAN POTTERS WERE MAKING COLORFUL GLASS BEADS. BUT GLASS WAS NOT USED TO MAKE WINDOWS UNTIL ABOUT 3,000 YEARS LATER. THE ROMANS DEVELOPED GREAT SKILLS IN GLASSMAKING AND BECAME THE FIRST PEOPLE TO HAVE GLAZED WINDOWS.

IT STILL TOOK UNTIL THE 16TH CENTURY FOR GLAZED WINDOWS TO BECOME A COMMON FEATURE IN HOUSES. POORER PEOPLE HAD TO DO WITHOUT GLASS WINDOWS FOR THREE MORE CENTURIES.

Connect!

THE DEVELOPMENT OF METAL FRAMES HAS MADE IT POSSIBLE TO MAKE BUILDINGS USING ENORMOUS PANES OF GLASS. SEE Q28.

Is stained glass really stained? IF SO, WITH WHAT?

Yes. To stain the glass, substances called metal oxides are added during the glassmaking process.

THE COLORFUL PIECES OF GLASS ARE HELD TOGETHER BY STRIPS OF LEAD. THE WINDOWS MAY TELL A STORY.

DIFFERENT OXIDES GIVE DIFFERENT COLORS.
ANTIMONY OXIDE = YELLOW
COBALT OXIDE = BLUE
COPPER OXIDE = RED
NICKEL OXIDE = PURPLE

← The stained glass windows in Lincoln Cathedral, England, record Lincoln's great fire in 1147.

Question 12

Do all windows open?

No. It depends on the style and function of the building.

The invention of air-conditioning means you no longer need to open a window to have ventilation. Windows should not open where it is unsafe or if valuable items behind the glass need to be protected.

THESE WINDOWS DO NOT OPEN...

STORE WINDOWS

WINDOWS IN HIGH-RISE OFFICE BUILDINGS

Connect! CAN NOT BEING ABLE TO OPEN A BUILDING'S WINDOWS AFFECT A PERSON'S HEALTH? SEE Q32.

Question

13 What is a doorway?

A doorway is made up of the door itself and the surrounding frame.

Like the first windows, early doors were simply openings in the building. They were made from animal skins and reeds and other plants. Today, nomads in Mongolia live in tentlike structures called yurts. The doors, made of felt, are opened by flipping them onto the roof.

PORTALS ARE PARTICULARLY GRAND DOORWAYS, WHICH MAY BE FOUND ON IMPRESSIVE PUBLIC BUILDINGS. THE COLOGNE CATHEDRAL, GERMANY, HAS AN IMPOSING GOTHIC PORTAL.

Look at these three doorways...

Guess which one belongs to:

A FAMILY HOME
A PRISON
A TEMPLE

THE ANSWERS ARE HIDDEN ON THIS PAGE.

1

2

3

Question

14 How do automatic doors work?

Automatic doors have a sensor above them. This detects any approaching people or objects.

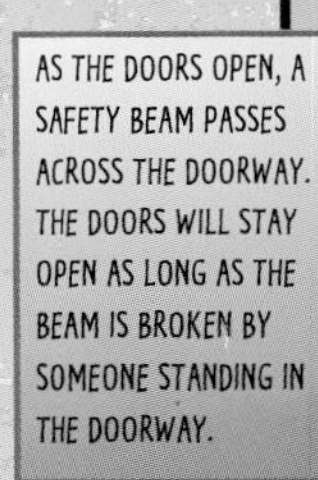

AS THE DOORS OPEN, A SAFETY BEAM PASSES ACROSS THE DOORWAY. THE DOORS WILL STAY OPEN AS LONG AS THE BEAM IS BROKEN BY SOMEONE STANDING IN THE DOORWAY.

THE SENSOR TRANSMITS MICROWAVES. THE PATTERN OF THESE IS CHANGED WHEN THEY BOUNCE OFF AN APPROACHING PERSON. THE ALTERED WAVES ARE REFLECTED BACK TO THE SENSOR, WHICH THEN KNOWS THAT SOMEONE IS IN THE AREA OF DETECTION. IT INSTRUCTS THE MOTOR TO OPEN THE DOORS.

☆ THE ANSWERS TO QUESTION 13 ARE: 1 IS A PRISON; 2 IS A TEMPLE; 3 IS A FAMILY HOME.

QUESTION

15 Why did people start building with stone?

Since early people moved around in search of food, the first buildings were probably temporary huts or tents, made from easily available natural materials, such as wood and animal skins. If these were scarce, or a more permanent shelter was required, stone was used.

The Egyptian pyramids at Giza are 4,000 years old. Each is made from about 2.5 million limestone blocks, one of which weighs around 2.5 tons.

☆ HOW WAS THIS POSSIBLE?

- There was a huge workforce, with armies of slaves quarrying and digging out the stone.
- There was an effective transportation system – the stone was moved to the site by transporting it on boats up the Nile River.

☆ WHY DO STONE WALLS ALL LOOK DIFFERENT?

BECAUSE THEY ARE MADE FROM MANY DIFFERENT KINDS OF ROCK.

1 SEDIMENTARY ROCK
Made of small particles of other rocks, sand, clay, and even animal skeletons.

SANDSTONE
SHALE
LIMESTONE →

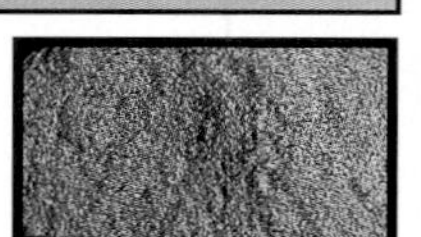

2 IGNEOUS ROCK
The heat from volcanoes causes underground rocks to melt. They set into different forms.

PUMICE
BASALT
GRANITE →

3 METAMORPHIC ROCK
Created by heat and pressure acting on sedimentary and igneous rock.

MARBLE →
ROCK FORMED FROM LIMESTONE
SLATE
ROCK FORMED FROM SHALE

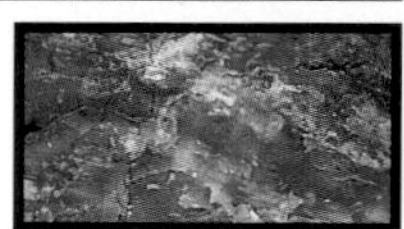

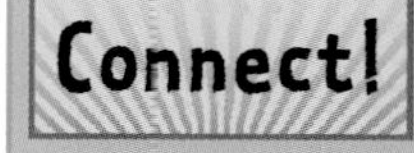

Connect! TODAY PEOPLE CONSTRUCT MAKESHIFT HOMES OUT OF ANY MATERIALS THEY CAN FIND. TURN TO Q27.

Connect! HOW DOES ACID RAIN AFFECT STONE BUILDINGS? SEE Q25.

QUESTION

16 Is concrete a new invention?

No! Read on.

Stones and bricks need something to hold them together. The most popular binding material, or mortar, is concrete – a mixture of cement, water, sand, and gravel – and it has been around for centuries.

☆ THE HISTORY OF CONCRETE

- **2ND CENTURY A.D.** THE ROMANS DISCOVER A VOLCANIC MINERAL WHICH THEY CALL POZZOLANA. THEY MIX THIS WITH LIME, GRAVEL, AND SAND TO MAKE A STRONGER MORTAR THAN THE LIME ONE ALREADY USED.
- **5TH TO 19TH CENTURY** THE FALL OF THE ROMAN EMPIRE RESULTS IN CONCRETE BEING FORGOTTEN FOR ALMOST FIFTEEN CENTURIES.
- **1824** CONCRETE IS REDISCOVERED WHEN BRITISH STONEMASON JOSEPH ASPDIN INVENTS PORTLAND CEMENT. IT REPLACES LIME AS ONE OF THE INGREDIENTS OF CONCRETE.
- **1850** FRENCH BUILDERS DISCOVER THAT CONCRETE CAN BE STRENGTHENED, OR REINFORCED, BY SETTING STEEL RODS IN IT.
- **1994** ASTRONAUTS ON THE SPACE SHUTTLE ENDEAVOUR TAKE PORTLAND CEMENT, SAND, AND WATER INTO SPACE. THEY ARE TRYING TO DISCOVER IF CONCRETE CAN BE SET IN THE WEIGHTLESS CONDITIONS OF SPACE.

Connect! TURN TO Q28 TO SEE THE EFFECT REINFORCED CONCRETE HAS HAD ON ARCHITECTURE.

Question 17: What is a brick?

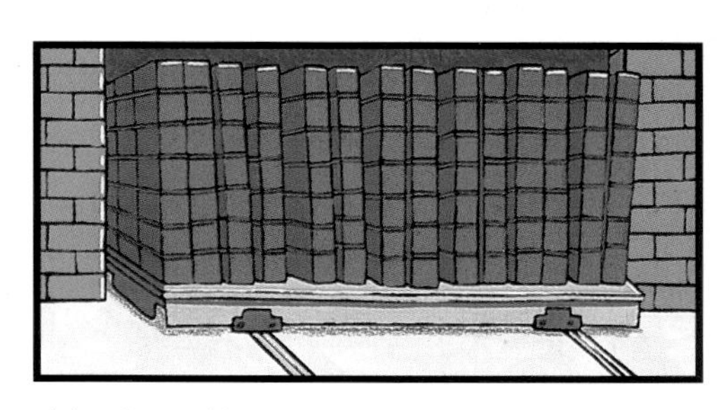

Unlike wood and stone, bricks are transformed materials – natural materials that have been altered by humans.

A brick is a block of clay that has been heated in a very hot oven, or kiln. Bricks may be red, white, or cream colored.

WHEN A BRICK WALL IS BUILT WHY ARE BRICKS NOT PLACED EXACTLY ON TOP OF EACH OTHER?

Bricks are commonly laid in a pattern known as a running bond. Each row of bricks overlaps the one below by half of its width. Arranging the bricks like this increases the strength of the wall. If the rows were simply stacked on top of each other, cracks would soon appear in the straight line of mortar running up the wall.

Prove It!

Collect together some rectangular cardboard boxes. Make one wall based on the pattern known as a "running bond," and a second with all the bricks stacked on top of each other. Which is the most stable?

Here are some of the ways bricks can be arranged...

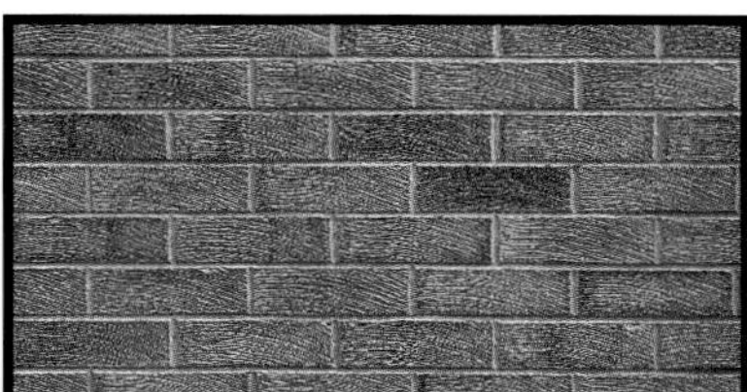

Question 18: What other materials can be used?

Take a look at these examples.

GLASS IT MAY LOOK FRAGILE, BUT GLASS CAN BE REMARKABLY STRONG WHEN ENCLOSED IN A FRAME. THIS GLASS PYRAMID IS THE ENTRANCE TO GALLERIES BENEATH THE LOUVRE MUSEUM IN PARIS, FRANCE.

SNOW IGLOOS ARE BUILT FROM SNOW BECAUSE IT IS OFTEN THE ONLY MATERIAL AVAILABLE. BLOCKS OF SNOW ARE LAID OUT IN A RISING SPIRAL PATTERN.

STRAW INSTEAD OF BRICKS THESE AMERICAN STRAW HOUSES ARE BUILT WITH BALES OF HAY. THESE ARE THEN COVERED WITH CEMENT AND STUCCO.

SCIENTISTS ARE EXPERIMENTING WITH A NEW BUILDING MATERIAL – A PLASTICLIKE SUBSTANCE EXTRACTED FROM THE SOYBEAN.

ARE ANY BUILDINGS MADE OF PLASTIC? Although there are over 10,000 types of plastic, there are two main problems with having plastic buildings.

1. Fires in buildings can reach temperatures of more than 1800°F, but no plastic can stand heat over 400°F.

2. Plastics give off dangerous fumes when they burn.

QUESTION

19 How can you tell when a building was

If you examine the architectural style, or look, of a building, you will find clues about when it was built.

TO DETERMINE THE ARCHITECTURAL STYLE OF A BUILDING, YOU NEED TO LOOK AT:

- The location – where it is built.
- The function – what it is used for.
- The design.
- The proportions – size, scale, shape.
- The materials and building techniques used.
- The ornamentation – how it is decorated.

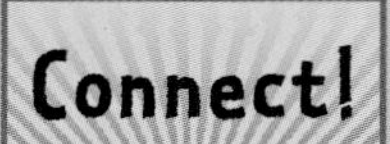

Connect! A BUILDING MAY BE MADE AS AN INDIVIDUAL'S FLIGHT OF FANCY. IT WILL NOT FIT INTO THIS HISTORICAL PATTERN. SEE Q23 AND Q29.

Your guide to the history of architecture

1 EGYPTIAN

FEATURES: Large stone constructions, often pyramids built in steps.
EXAMPLE: Pyramid of Cheops, Giza, Egypt (2723–2563 B.C.).

2 CLASSICAL GREEK

FEATURES: Stone temples, with curved or sculpted columns.
EXAMPLE: Parthenon, Athens, Greece (447–436 B.C.).

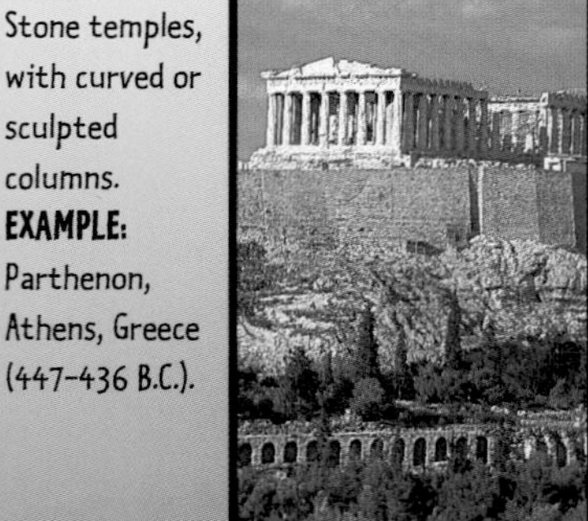

9 BAROQUE

FEATURES: Very ornate, grand buildings, with many columns, windows, and sweeping curves.
EXAMPLE: Santa Maria del Salute, Venice, Italy (1631–1682).

10 NEOCLASSIC

FEATURES: A revival of Ancient Roman and Greek styles, using symmetry, columns, and pediments (triangular roof crowns).
EXAMPLE: Massachusetts State House, Boston (1793).

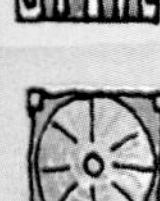

11 GOTHIC REVIVAL

FEATURES: Elaborate Gothic-style windows, walls, and towers.
EXAMPLE: Houses of Parliament, London, England (1840–1860).

12 METAL CONSTRUCTION

FEATURES: Skeleton made of steel or cast iron, with glass and ornamental decoration.
EXAMPLE: Crystal Palace, London, England (1851).

13 BAROQUE REVIVAL

FEATURES: Double columns, oval pediments, and sculpture as part of design.
EXAMPLE: Paris Opera House, Paris, France (1861–1874).

made just by looking at it?

3 CLASSICAL ROMAN

FEATURES: Oval shape, made up of a series of arches on several levels.
EXAMPLE: Colosseum, Rome, Italy (70–82).

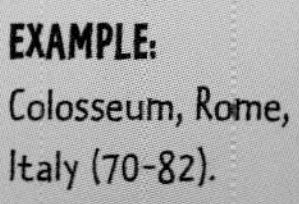

4 EARLY CHRISTIAN

FEATURES: Main building in center, with columns inside and flat walls outside.
EXAMPLE: San Vitale, Ravenna, Italy (526–547).

5 EARLY ISLAMIC

FEATURES: Spiral tower, with flat or domed roof held up by columns.
EXAMPLE: Great Mosque of Samarra, Iraq (848–852).

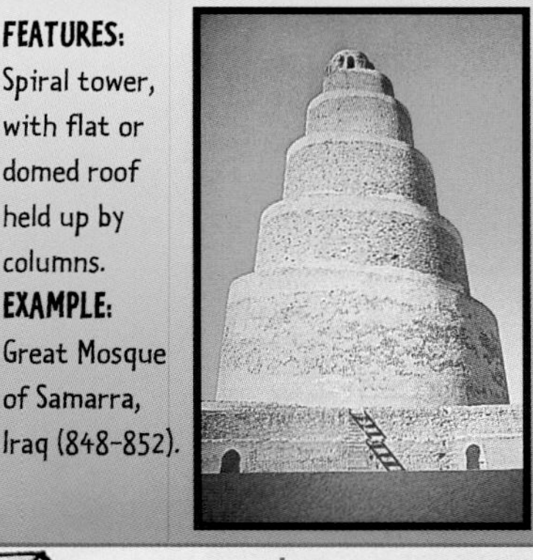

6 ROMANESQUE

FEATURES: Large castlelike main building, with round arch windows.
EXAMPLE: Tower of London, England (1078–90).

7 GOTHIC

FEATURES: Elaborate wall decorations and sculptures, with spires and stained glass.
EXAMPLE: Notre Dame Cathedral, Paris, France (1163–1250).

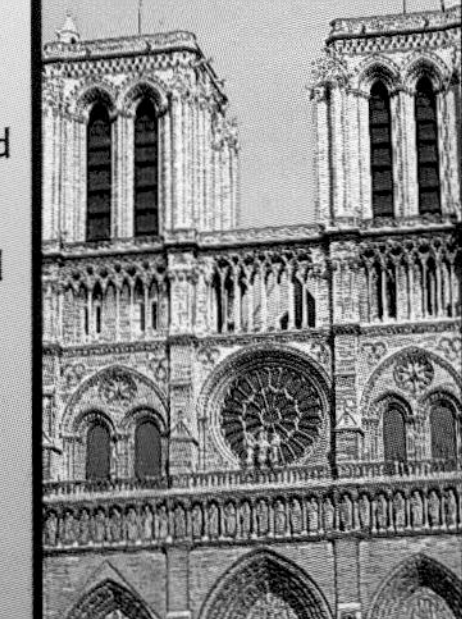

8 RENAISSANCE

FEATURES: Very symmetrical and in proportion, with good use of curves and straight lines.
EXAMPLE: Pazzi Chapel, Florence, Italy (around 1400).

14 INTERNATIONAL

FEATURES: Reinforced concrete slabs, with white walls, flat roofs, and large windows.
EXAMPLE: Melnikov's House, Moscow, Russia (1927).

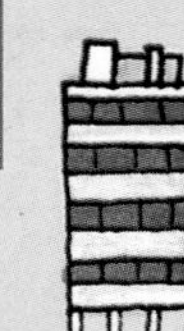

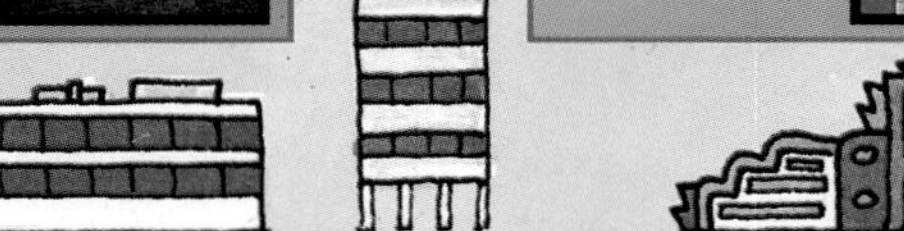

15 ART DECO

FEATURES: Simple but bold geometric building shapes and decoration.
EXAMPLE: Chrysler Building, New York City (1928–1930).

16 HIGH TECH

FEATURES: The structure and working parts of the building are left visible.
EXAMPLE: Hongkong and Shanghai Banking Corporation Headquarters, Statue Square, Hong Kong (1986).

Connect!

WHAT'S NEXT? TURN TO Q35 TO FIND OUT.

Prove It!

Take a look at the buildings in your own area. What style do they fit into? How many share features of two or more styles?

20 How is a house built?

In different countries different techniques are used and much depends on the materials.

Here's a common sequence for building a brick house.

Lay strong foundations for the house to rest on. Dig deep trenches where the walls will go and fill with concrete.

Construct the brick walls. Leave spaces for windows and doors.

Moving on up, erect wooden frameworks for ceilings and floors. These will support the floorboards and ceilings.

Make the roof from a similar timber framework and cover with roofing materials such as tiles or slate.

Fit windows and doors and build a staircase. The house is now a waterproof shell, allowing builders to work inside.

Now, install wiring and then plaster the ceilings and lay down floorboards.

Install the plumbing, lifting floorboards or drilling through plaster, where necessary. Attach power outlets and light switches.

Why are buildings demolished?

The materials used to make a building may start to wear away. For safety reasons, the building is demolished. Others are demolished because different buildings on the same site would have more value.

MANY HOUSES BUILT IN THE INDUSTRIAL REVOLUTION, AROUND THE MID-18TH CENTURY, ARE NOW DILAPIDATED AND UNCOMFORTABLE TO LIVE IN.

HOW THE VAN ECK HOUSE SKYSCRAPER IN SOUTH AFRICA FELL TO EARTH IN 1983.

GOING... Almost 2,000 explosive charges are drilled into the walls and columns of the building.

GOING... As the charges explode upward through the 20 stories, the skyscraper collapses.

GONE! In just sixteen seconds, the building is reduced to a pile of rubble.

QUESTION

Why does the Leaning Tower of Pisa lean (and will it ever topple over)?

← Pisa's famous tower has been leaning for more than 800 years, because the foundations beneath the tower are not strong enough to support its weight evenly. The tower moves a further 0.06 in. each year. If nothing is done, it will eventually come crashing down. As a temporary measure, heavy counterbalancing weights have been placed on the ground at one side of the tower.

Connections!

PART 2

ugly, weird, wonderful...

Why do buildings look like they do?

How does a building's use affect what it looks like?

What is a folly?

Can the weather damage the structure of a building?

The journey continues. Just turn the page and you will discover in PART TWO what factors are taken into consideration when a building is being planned.

Question 23

How does the use of a building affect what it ends up looking like?

Some buildings give you strong clues as to what they are used for. Their design helps them carry out certain functions.

LARGE GLASS TOP SENDS OUT A NARROW BEAM OF LIGHT WHICH CAN SWEEP AROUND IN A CIRCLE.

CYLINDRICAL, TALL STRUCTURE ALLOWS GOOD VIEWS OF THE COAST AND THE SEA.

A LIGHTHOUSE

LARGE VANES OR SAILS TURN AS THE WIND BLOWS. THESE ARE ATTACHED TO A SHAFT, WHICH IN TURN MOVES A STONE FOR GRINDING CORN, OR A WATER PUMP.

SOME MILLS **ROTATE** ON A VERTICAL POST, SO THAT THEY CAN CHANGE DIRECTION AS THE WIND DOES.

A WINDMILL

Sometimes it is hard to believe buildings are actually buildings – they look so strange!

NORMAN HOUSE, OKLAHOMA, 1961. THIS EXTRAORDINARY PRAIRIE HOUSE, DESIGNED BY THE ARCHITECT HERB GREENE, LOOKS LIKE A CROSS BETWEEN A SLIDE AND A GARBAGE DUMP. IT IS BASED ON THE RAMSHACKLE BUILDINGS FOUND IN A SHANTYTOWN.

HOMES IN THE NETHERLANDS THE DUTCH ARCHITECT PIET BLOM DREW INSPIRATION FROM TREE HOUSES WHEN HE DESIGNED THESE TOPSY-TURVY HOMES. THESE ODD-LOOKING BUILDINGS ARE ONLY MADE POSSIBLE BY THE POWER OF REINFORCED CONCRETE.

U.S. PAVILION, MONTREAL EXPO, CANADA, 1967. THIS ENORMOUS DOME, DESIGNED BY RICHARD BUCKMINSTER FULLER, IS MADE FROM LIGHTWEIGHT STEEL AND ACRYLIC PANELS. THE ARCHITECT HAD A VISION OF COVERING WHOLE CITIES WITH SUCH DOMES.

Prove It!

It is not always easy to guess a building's function. What do you think this building is used for?

☆ THE ANSWER IS HIDDEN ON THE NEXT PAGE.

Connect!

OVER THE CENTURIES, ARCHITECTS WITH STRONG PERSONAL VISIONS HAVE REVOLUTIONIZED BUILDING STYLES. SEE Q29.

Do some buildings have no obvious or practical use?

A folly may be built for ornamental reasons. It may be a way of fulfilling an individual's fantasy or dream. The structure gets its name because of the owner's apparent foolishness, or "folly," in building it.

Woodbridge Lodge, Suffolk, England, was built around 1800. The folly has strong Gothic influences.

BATTLEMENTS AND NARROW WINDOWS ALLOWED ARCHERS TO AIM OUTWARD, WHILE OFFERING PROTECTION.

MASSIVE WALLS AND TOWERS ARE TOO THICK AND TALL TO BE DESTROYED BY ENEMY ATTACK.

Connect! SOME BUILDING DESIGNS ARE INFLUENCED BY THE FASHION OF THE TIME. TURN TO Q26.

QUESTION

How does the location of a building affect its design?

Location is always considered. In high-risk earthquake areas, such as San Francisco and Tokyo, buildings are specially made to try and cope with quake conditions.

1 LOWER BUILDINGS ARE MADE FROM LIGHTWEIGHT MATERIALS TO MINIMIZE THE DAMAGE TO THE SURROUNDING AREA IF THEY COLLAPSE IN AN EARTHQUAKE.

2 TALLER BUILDINGS HAVE FLEXIBLE INTERNAL SUPPORTS, ALLOWING THEM TO MOVE WITH THE FORCE OF THE EARTHQUAKE WITHOUT BREAKING.

THE SIX-STORY NUNOTANI OFFICE BUILDING IN TOKYO, JAPAN, IS STURDIER THAN IT LOOKS. ITS SLOPING WALLS, CEILINGS, AND FLOORS ARE DESIGNED TO WITHSTAND DESTRUCTION BY AN EARTHQUAKE.

Connect! TURN TO Q25 TO SEE WHAT EFFECT THE CLIMATE OF AN AREA CAN HAVE ON THE LOOK OF THE BUILDING.

☆ THE MYSTERY BUILDING IS A CATHEDRAL IN TOKYO, JAPAN.

How does climate affect what a building looks like?

Buildings around the world are made in all shapes and sizes – from Japanese pagodas and Indian temples to Arctic log cabins. One reason for this variety is because buildings must cope with local weather conditions.

ASK YOURSELF...

IS IT SUNNY?

Buildings in hot places need to provide shade from the sun. They may do this by having:

1. Thick walls and small windows to keep out the heat.
2. Whitewashed walls, which reflect the heat.

THE PARAPORTIANI CHURCH IN MYKONOS TOWN, GREECE.

IS IT WET?

Buildings in areas of high rainfall need to avoid being damaged by torrential rain. They may be built:

1. On stilts, to stand clear of floodwater.
2. With sloping roofs and a gutter system to take away excess rain.

STILTED HOUSES ON THE EQUATOR, NEAR SAMARINDA, KALIMANTAN, INDONESIA.

Buildings in cold areas need to keep out the cold and store heat. They may do this by:

1. The use of materials such as wood. Timber buildings warm up more quickly than brick ones.
2. Having sloping roofs to keep off excess snow.

A SKI CHALET IN SWITZERLAND IN THE WINTER.

CASE STUDY 1

KEEPING COOL

HOUSES IN PLACES THAT HAVE HOT SUMMERS ARE OFTEN BUILT AROUND A COURTYARD. ALMOST ALL THE ROOMS LOOK OUT ONTO THE COURTYARD. HERE THE AIR IS COOL, SINCE THE OUTER WALLS SHIELD THE YARD FROM THE SUN. THE FEW WINDOWS IN THE BUILDING TEND TO BE SMALL AND OFTEN HAVE SHUTTERS TO SHADE THEM.

The open courtyard design is particularly popular in Mediterranean countries, such as Spain, Greece, and Italy.

CASE STUDY 2

SNOWED UNDER

THE LATEST BRITISH RESEARCH STATION TO BRAVE THE FREEZING CONDITIONS OF THE ANTARCTIC IS CALLED HALLEY 5. STEEL LEGS RAISE THE STATION BUILDINGS 15 FT INTO THE AIR. AT THIS HEIGHT, THE GALE FORCE ANTARCTIC WINDS EASILY BLOW AWAY SNOW RESTING ON THE ROOF.

Halley 5 took six years to be designed and built. Previous stations in the Antarctic had not been able to withstand the severe weather.

Can the climate directly affect the structure of a building?

YES! HERE ARE FOUR WAYS WEATHER CONDITIONS ACT ON BUILDINGS

1 WIND

The power of the wind should not be underestimated. The wind may be invisible, but the impact it can have is not.

In 1989, thousands of buildings were destroyed after Hurricane Hugo swept from the coast of Africa to North Carolina.

SWAYING SKYSCRAPERS

The higher up you go the stronger the wind becomes. Winds blowing at the top of a 100-story skyscraper are four times more powerful than those halfway down. Not surprisingly, tall buildings actually start swaying in very windy conditions.

The Royal and Commerce Bank Building in Toronto, Canada.

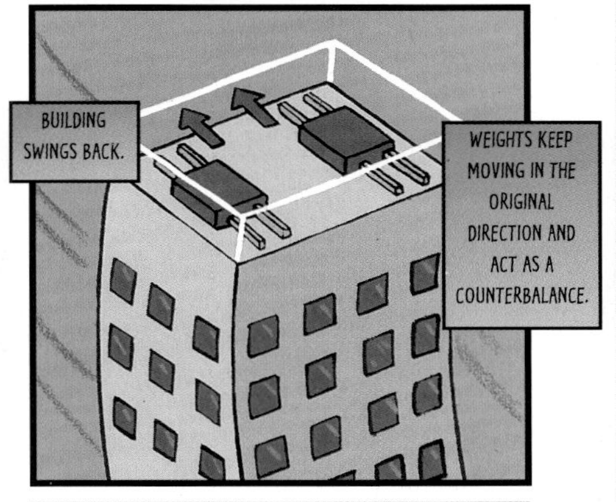

One way of reducing sway is to mount large weights on rollers at the top of the building.

2 TEMPERATURE

Sudden temperature changes cause concrete buildings to crack. This problem occurs when water seeps into the tiny cracks already present in concrete.

- AS THE TEMPERATURE FALLS, THE WATER TURNS TO ICE.
- BECAUSE WATER EXPANDS AS IT FREEZES, THE CRACK BECOMES BIGGER.
- THE ICE MELTS, ONLY TO FREEZE AGAIN THE NEXT NIGHT.
- THE CRACK KEEPS GETTING BIGGER.

THE FREEZE-THAW CYCLE CAN EXPOSE THE STEEL RODS USED TO REINFORCE CONCRETE.

3 RAIN

When rain mixes with pollutant gases in the air such as sulfur dioxide, it falls to the ground as acid rain. This dissolves calcium carbonate, which is the main ingredient of limestone and sandstone.

Acid rain causes buildings to crumble and wear away.

Prove It!

Rain also seeps into timber. The cells in the wood absorb the water and swell up. Test it out by trying to open a wooden door after a rainy period. Don't be surprised if it's stuck. The extra moisture in the cells has made the door grow in size.

4 ATMOSPHERE

Some buildings actually change color. A process called oxidation makes copper roofs turn blue-green. This coating, or patina, is a result of substances in the atmosphere acting on the copper. The patina is good for the building, as it forms a protective barrier that stops further corrosion.

The domed entrance gate of Hofburg Imperial Palace in Vienna, Austria, has a copper roof.

QUESTION

26 Can fashion affect the look of a building?

If you look back to the architectural journey we made in question 19, you'll see that building styles have often been influenced by the trends or events of the time.

Art Deco

Art Deco was the style of the Jazz Age. It took its name from a decorative arts exhibition in Paris in 1925.

Berkeley Shore Hotel, Miami, Florida (1940).
ARCHITECT: ALBERT ANIS.
The entrance and front of this building feature many geometric designs and decorations

The simple, bold, and bright designs of Art Deco, with their geometric patterns and sharp edges, suggested luxury and sophistication. The style influenced everything from clothes and furnishings to book covers and haircuts.

Modernist De Stijl

The Dutch De Stijl group was founded in 1917. They were early followers of the Modernist movement, which believed that buildings should look as simple and boxlike as possible. They did not like decoration.

THE DE STIJL MOVEMENT WAS INFLUENCED BY THE WORK OF ABSTRACT PAINTER PIET MONDRIAN.

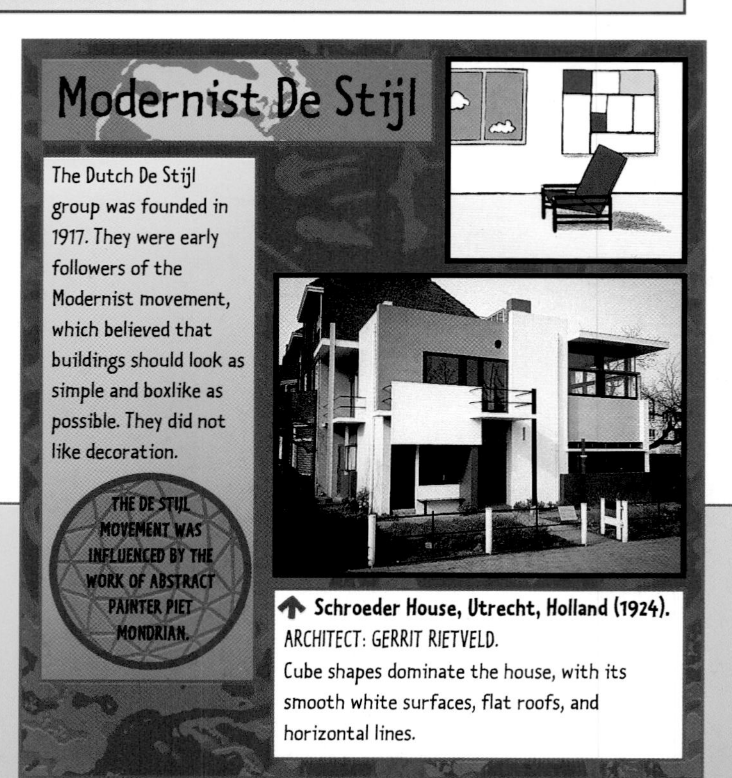

Schroeder House, Utrecht, Holland (1924).
ARCHITECT: GERRIT RIETVELD.
Cube shapes dominate the house, with its smooth white surfaces, flat roofs, and horizontal lines.

Metro-land

In the early 20th century, London's underground subway network started to reach out into the fringes of the capital. New suburbs grew around the stations. In 1915, the term "Metro-land" was invented to describe these new areas. The houses in Metro-land were often built in a romantic, Tudor style to reflect the wealth and comfort of the suburb.

THIS METRO-LAND GUIDE WAS PRODUCED ANNUALLY BY THE METROPOLITAN RAILWAY BETWEEN 1915 AND 1932. IT WAS INTENDED TO ENCOURAGE PEOPLE TO BUY HOUSES IN THE NEW SUBURBS.

Connect!

TURN TO Q28 TO SEE HOW TECHNOLOGICAL DEVELOPMENTS AND INVENTIONS CHANGED THE WAY BUILDINGS COULD BE MADE.

Question

27 What about the space, the materials, and the money available?

☆ MEAGER MATERIALS

Around some large cities, such as in India and South America, people live in shanty-towns. They cannot afford to rent or buy homes, so they have to build their own. The houses are very basic and are made from whatever materials are available.

Many shanty houses are built from sheets of corrugated iron.

☆ THE MOST EXPENSIVE HOUSE

The view across the Neptune Pool of the Hearst Ranch.

The Hearst Ranch at San Simeon, California, is the most expensive house ever built. It cost $30 million in 1922 and took 17 years to complete. It has more than 100 rooms, a swimming pool, and a garage large enough to park 25 limousines.

☆ SPACED OUT

The height of a building may depend on where it is constructed. If land is expensive or if there is not much land available, buildings tend to be taller. Where land is cheap and there is plenty of it, buildings do not have to be high-rise and can be sprawling.

PLACE: HONG KONG.
AREA: 415 SQUARE MI.
POPULATION: 5,800,000.
DENSITY: 13,976 PEOPLE TO EVERY SQUARE MI.
BUILDING: SKYSCRAPERS CAN HOUSE UP TO 1,000 PEOPLE.

PLACE: CANBERRA, AUSTRALIA.
AREA: 927 SQUARE MI.
POPULATION: 273,600.
DENSITY: 295 PEOPLE TO EVERY SQUARE MI.
BUILDING: SPACIOUS HOUSES ACCOMMODATE VERY FEW PEOPLE.

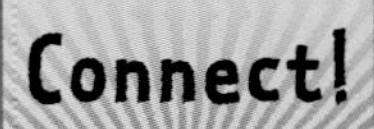

Connect! HOW DO DIFFERENT BUILDINGS AFFECT THE WAY WE FEEL? SEE Q31.

Connect! TURN TO Q34 TO FIND OUT WHY SOME HIGH-RISE BUILDINGS DID NOT LIVE UP TO EXPECTATIONS.

Beware! The look of a building can be deceptive. Some buildings look so out of place you wonder how they got there. Take a look at these two photographs. Can you guess by looking at the buildings in which country you will find them?

The Royal Pavilion, built between 1815 and 1818, may look Indian, but is, in fact, found in Brighton, England. It was designed by John Nash for the Prince Regent, George IV. The exotic Eastern look was inspired by the Mogul buildings of Delhi.

This is not an Italian village – it is **Portmeirion** in Gwynedd, Wales. These Mediterranean-looking buildings were built between 1933 and 1972 by Clough Ellis, a wealthy eccentric. He wanted the Welsh town to look like a port in Italy.

Connect! REMEMBER THE FOLLIES IN Q23? WELL, IF YOU TURN TO Q29, YOU'LL READ ABOUT A MAN WHO CREATED THE STRANGEST LOOKING BUILDINGS IN THE WORLD – ANTONIO GAUDI.

Question 28 How have inventions changed the way buildings look?

Building techniques have been greatly influenced by one major event – the Industrial Revolution in the 18th century. It began in Britain around 1760 and soon spread to the rest of Europe and America. Machines were invented to produce goods on a grand scale, large factories sprang up, and new building materials were discovered.

Charting the changes

1779

THE WORLD'S FIRST CAST-IRON BRIDGE WAS ERECTED IN SHROPSHIRE, ENGLAND. ITS SUCCESS ENCOURAGED PEOPLE TO EXPERIMENT AND USE METAL IN THE STRUCTURE OF BUILDINGS.

1803

RICHARD TREVITHICK BUILT THE FIRST RAILROAD LOCOMOTIVE. THIS NEW FORM OF TRANSPORTATION ALLOWED RAW MATERIALS, SUCH AS COAL, TO BE MOVED QUICKLY TO AND FROM THE FACTORY.

1856

HENRY BESSEMER DISCOVERED A CHEAP WAY OF TURNING IRON INTO STEEL. THIS WAS STRONGER AND LONGER-LASTING THAN IRON AND BECAME THE FAVORED METAL IN BUILDING CONSTRUCTION.

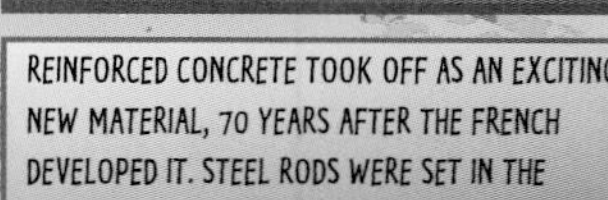

1920s

REINFORCED CONCRETE TOOK OFF AS AN EXCITING NEW MATERIAL, 70 YEARS AFTER THE FRENCH DEVELOPED IT. STEEL RODS WERE SET IN THE CONCRETE TO GIVE IT GREATER STRENGTH.

Connect! WHAT MAJOR CHANGES CAN WE EXPECT IN THE FUTURE? CHECK OUT Q35.

Why does modern architecture look like it does?

One reason is that reinforced concrete is an incredibly versatile material. It can be cast into almost any shape, even those which seem to defy gravity.

THE ARCHITECT FRANK LLOYD WRIGHT ACTUALLY DEMONSTRATED THE BALANCING QUALITY OF REINFORCED CONCRETE BY STANDING UNDERNEATH A HORIZONTAL JUTTING-OUT SLAB, CALLED A CANTILEVER. ONCE IT HAD SET, HE KICKED AWAY THE TIMBER SUPPORTS HOLDING IT IN PLACE. THE BUILDERS BREATHED A SIGH OF RELIEF WHEN THE CANTILEVER REMAINED HORIZONTAL AND DID NOT COME CRASHING DOWN.

☆ STEEL SKELETONS

The walls of a house support the whole building. They keep up the floors, ceilings, and roof. In a skyscraper, there is too much weight for ordinary walls to bear, so skyscrapers are built around a steel or concrete frame. This is light in weight but strong enough to support the floors, walls, and enormous panes of glass.

Question

29 How have some architects influenced style and form?

Some individuals have had strong dreams and visions. Their ideas have revolutionized the way we view buildings. Here are just a few of the great architects.

CHRISTOPHER WREN

(1632–1723)

FAMOUS FOR: ST. PAUL'S CATHEDRAL, LONDON, ENGLAND (1675–1710).

WREN WAS CHOSEN TO REBUILD THE CATHEDRAL AFTER IT WAS DESTROYED IN THE GREAT FIRE OF LONDON IN 1666.

ANTONIO GAUDI

(1852–1926)

FAMOUS FOR: CASA BATLLO, BARCELONA, SPAIN (1907).

GAUDI REMODELED THE FACADE OF THESE APARTMENTS INTO A BIZARRE EXTRAVAGANZA COMPLETE WITH REPTILIAN SCALES.

LE CORBUSIER

(1887–1965)

FAMOUS FOR: NOTRE DAME DU HAUT, RONCHAMP, FRANCE (1950–55).

LE CORBUSIER DESIGNED THIS CATHEDRAL SO THAT IT WOULD APPEAR INTERESTING FROM WHICHEVER ANGLE IT WAS VIEWED.

FRANK LLOYD WRIGHT

(1869–1959)

FAMOUS FOR: FALLING WATER, PENNSYLVANIA (1937–39).

THIS CONCRETE MASTERPIECE IS THE REALIZATION OF WRIGHT'S DREAM TO DESIGN BUILDINGS THAT FITTED IN WITH THEIR SURROUNDINGS.

The steel framework is clearly visible on this half-built New York skyscraper.

☆ HIGHER AND HIGHER

New engineering techniques are making it possible to construct increasingly taller buildings. The glass-paneled Tour Sans Fins will be built in Paris using reinforced concrete, which makes a stiffer frame than steel.

At 1,398 ft tall, the Tour Sans Fins will be the tallest building in Europe. The Empire State Building in New York City measures 1,250 ft.

Connect!

SOME TECHNOLOGICAL ADVANCES HAVE MADE BUILDINGS "SICK." WHAT DOES THIS MEAN? SEE Q32.

Connect!

CAN YOU BUILD WHAT YOU LIKE, WHEREVER YOU LIKE? TURN TO Q30 TO FIND OUT MORE.

Connect!

ARCHITECTS MAY HAVE EXTRAORDINARY DREAMS, BUT PEOPLE HAVE TO USE THEIR BUILDINGS. TURN TO Q34 TO FIND OUT MORE.

QUESTION 30

Can you just build what you like where you like?

Erecting a new building usually involves more than just laying bricks wherever you choose. People must follow the building codes and zoning regulations of the area.

What is a building code?

This is a set of rules that must be followed in constructing a building. The main considerations are health and safety. Most cities have a building inspector whose job it is to enforce the building code, for example, to make sure that there are at least two safe exits from a building in case of fire.

BUILDING CODES REQUIRE THE NEW PROPERTY TO...

- ✓ BE SAFE AND STRUCTURALLY SOUND.
- ✓ BE A HEALTHY PLACE TO LIVE IN.
- ✓ ALLOW PEOPLE EASY ACCESS IN AND OUT.
- ✓ FIT IN WITH THE SURROUNDING BUILDINGS.
- ✓ NOT BLOCK ANY ROADS OR CAUSE AN OBSTRUCTION.
- ✓ BE THE RIGHT HEIGHT.

ZONING REGULATIONS DETERMINE WHAT THE LAND IN AN AREA CAN BE USED FOR AND WHAT KINDS OF BUILDINGS CAN BE CONSTRUCTED.

In ancient Babylon, architects were sentenced to death if one of their buildings collapsed and killed someone.

THIS HOUSE IS IN A CONSERVATION AREA IN ENGLAND. THIS MEANS THE OCCUPIER MUST SEEK PERMISSION TO CHANGE THE CHARACTER OF THE PROPERTY. THE DEVELOPMENT OF THE AREA IS OFTEN RESTRICTED BY THE LOCAL AUTHORITY.

Connect! HOW DO ARCHITECTS DESIGN BUILDINGS FOR DISABLED PEOPLE? SEE Q31.

CASE STUDY → The Globe Theater

Around 400 years ago, William Shakespeare's plays were performed at the Globe Theater, in London. But on June 29, 1613 tragedy struck. During a performance of Henry VIII, a cannon was fired that accidentally set the thatched roof ablaze. The theater was burned to the ground.

Building codes mean the new Globe Theater has a number of fire exits, a water sprinkler in the roof, and a waterproof thatch.

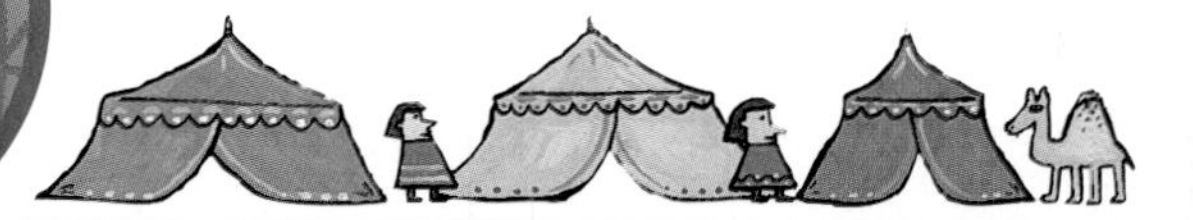

Keeping on the move...

Nomads are wandering travelers. They move from one place to another in search of water and grazing land for their animals. Nomads need shelters that are temporary, light, and portable.

The Bedouin tribe are nomadic Arabs, who live in waterproof tents woven from goat hair.

Connections!

buildings...

How do they affect the people who use them and the space around them?

Can buildings really change the way we feel?

Do buildings ever get sick?

What will buildings look like in the future?

Buildings should be designed to be used and enjoyed by the people that move in and out of them every day. PART THREE takes a look at why some buildings are successful and others are not.

QUESTION

31 How do different buildings make us feel?

People may have different reactions when they are asked to comment on a variety of architectural styles. This will depend on many factors.

Look at these buildings and choose the word that you feel best describes them.

AN ENGLISH TERRACED HOUSE

COMFORTABLE?
BORING?
UNADVENTUROUS?
FUNCTIONAL?

A FRENCH CHATEAU

REGAL?
RICH?
UNFRIENDLY?
MAGNIFICENT?

A NORWEGIAN LAPP TENT

FUN?
COLD?
FRAGILE?
SIMPLE?

A JAPANESE SKYSCRAPER

UGLY?
MODERN?
FUTURISTIC?
BUSINESSLIKE?

QUESTION

32 What is building sickness?

Some buildings can make you ill. This is called "sick building syndrome."

Why do some buildings make people sick? → Buildings may have windows that do not open, and if the building is ventilated artificially, such as by air-conditioning, this may mean that germs and stagnant air end up lingering in the building for a long time.

What are the symptoms of sick building syndrome? →

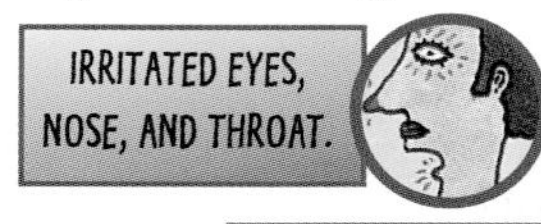

MEMORY LOSS AND REDUCED CONCENTRATION.

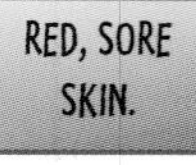

RED, SORE SKIN.

How can architects make life easier for disabled people?

PEOPLE WHO USE WHEELCHAIRS

Getting around an ordinary building can be hard work for someone who is in a wheelchair. Stairs, narrow corridors, and swinging doors turn into obstacles. Architects have had to think more carefully when they design public buildings to ensure that everyone who wants to use them can.

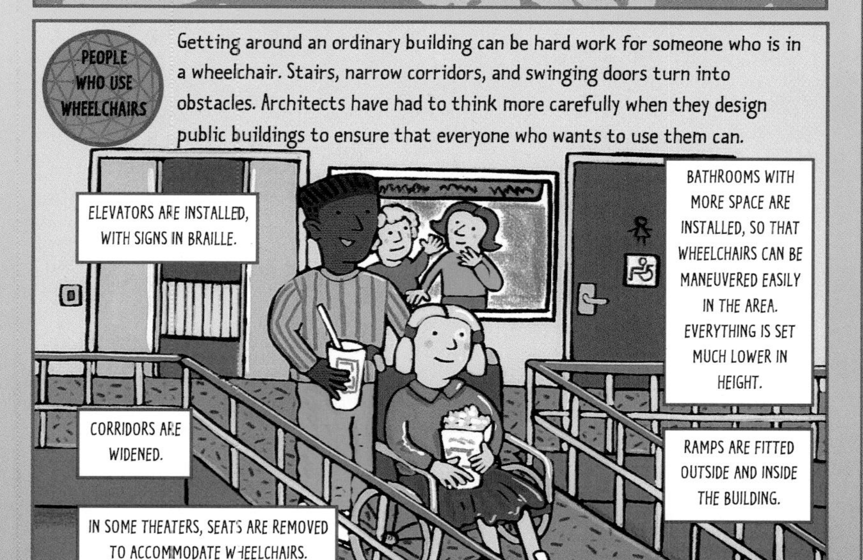

PEOPLE WITH VISUAL IMPAIRMENTS

If you have poor eyesight, making your way around a building can be very confusing. The Royal National Institute for the Blind has specially designed its college in Loughborough, England, to show how a building can be adapted to make it easier for visually impaired people.

FLOORS ARE PAVED IN DIFFERENT MATERIALS. WALKING ON THE VARIOUS SURFACES MAKES A VARIETY OF NOISES AND LETS STUDENTS HEAR THAT THEY ARE IN A DIFFERENT PART OF THE BUILDING.

THE EDGES OF DOORS AND HANDLES ARE PAINTED IN STRONG, BRIGHT COLORS TO STAND OUT FROM THE REST OF THE BUILDING.

GUIDE RAILS AND BARS ARE ATTACHED TO THE WALLS.

SIGNS ARE WRITTEN IN LARGE, CLEAR, RAISED TYPE.

Prove It!

Sit in a chair in your home and list the difficulties you would face every day if you could not walk, see, or hear.

What is geopathic stress?

Some people believe buildings can suffer from a condition called "geopathic stress." Buildings are said to receive negative energies caused by underground streams crossing over. The streams are said to send out radiation, which rises up from the ground and passes through the property.

In China, people may go around to check the energies of the land before any new building is constructed.

QUESTION

33 Is our opinion of a building changed by what it is next to?

Look at these two photographs. Both feature tall buildings. But do we feel the same way about those buildings? Examine the varying opinions below.

☆ CANARY WHARF TOWER IN LONDON

1 **OPINION:** THE TALL BUILDING IS AN EYESORE. IT HAS DESTROYED THE CHARACTER OF THE SURROUNDING AREA.

2 **OPINION:** THE TALL BUILDING IS A GRAND ARCHITECTURAL STATEMENT THAT HAS BROUGHT NEW LIFE TO THE AREA.

☆ ABERDEEN HARBOR IN HONG KONG

1 **OPINION:** TALL BUILDINGS ARE COMMON IN HONG KONG. THE BUILDING FITS IN EFFORTLESSLY. ITS HEIGHT IS ACCEPTABLE.

2 **OPINION:** TOO MANY HIGH-RISE BUILDINGS IN ONE AREA MAKE A CITY CLAUSTROPHOBIC AND UNWELCOMING.

Connect!

WHAT NEXT? WILL BUILDINGS GET TALLER AND TALLER? CHECK OUT Q35.

QUESTION 34

Can a building fail?

Not all buildings have been successes. Some have failed because they did not suit the needs of the people they housed. Others have failed because they were structurally unsound.

Prove It!

Look around your house. Are there parts of it that don't work very well? What would you change to make it function better?

FAILED – THE USERS' NEEDS NOT MET

THE PRUITT-IGOE HOUSING PROJECT

This housing development in St. Louis, Missouri, aimed to give residents "streets in the air." Instead, people felt lonely and isolated in the 14-story buildings. The buildings were dynamited to the ground just 17 years later.

FAILED – STRUCTURALLY UNSOUND

RONAN POINT HOUSING ESTATE

On May 16, 1968, a leaking gas stove in one apartment of this project in London, England, caused a massive explosion, blowing out the external load-bearing wall. This resulted in the collapse of part of the block. After being rebuilt with reinforced concrete it was still thought unsafe and was demolished in 1986.

How do you make stronger building materials?

One way is to test what happens to materials under severe pressure.

This sequence of pictures shows a jet fighter plane crashing into a concrete block. American scientists then compared the results of the impact with a computer prediction to see how accurate it was. The information helps them to develop stronger materials.

0.0 secs An unmanned F-4 Phantom zooms in toward the block.

0.02 secs Special equipment and cameras record the nose hitting the wall at 480 mph.

0.1 sec The plane goes up in flames. The experiment tells the scientists vital information about the construction of concrete.

Success!

THE POMPIDOU CENTER – A USER-FRIENDLY DESIGN AND A GOOD USE OF SPACE

The Pompidou Center, built in Paris between 1972 and 1977, was designed by Piano and Rogers. The building is a success because, by placing all the engineering elements – like escalators and ventilation systems – on the outside, the designers allowed more space on the inside for exhibitions and displays. They also created a revolutionary looking building that drew people to the place and encouraged them to enjoy the cultural events that were taking place inside.

Question

35 What will buildings be like in the future?

Our changing lifestyles and growing populations will greatly influence future building design. As land gets used up, there will be two main options for easing the overcrowding.

1 GOING UP...

Buildings of the future are likely to reach for the sky. They will contain everything from offices, living space, shops, movie theaters, and restaurants.

TOWERING TOKYO

Land in Tokyo, Japan, is the most expensive in the world. The area covered by the Imperial Palace in Tokyo is worth more than the whole of California. So building upward makes economic sense.

The Millennium Tower is due to be built in Tokyo in the near future. At 2,625 ft, it will be almost twice as tall as Sears Tower, the world's current tallest building.

2 GOING DOWN...

Building down is ideal for buildings that do not need daylight in order to function; for example, movie theaters. Underground buildings are easy to heat and do not spoil the environment above.

SUNKEN CITIES

Architects in Japan are considering plans for an underground city called Geotropolis. It would exist 160 ft below the surface, and have its own road and rail networks. Large skylights would contain rotating prisms, which would follow the sun and reflect light down onto underground gardens.

Geotropolis looks fine on paper, but its design is revolutionary. No one knows the effect an underground city like this would have on its inhabitants.

What else might happen?

In some areas, like the Arizona desert, people live in domes. The pleasant, comfortable conditions in the dome remain unchanged, so you could be anywhere in the world.

How do you build an Earth within the earth? Make a huge self-contained glass bubble, of course! For two years, scientists lived in Biosphere 2, Arizona, without ever stepping outside.

Connections!

In the future will we still need buildings for public gatherings and office workers? Advances in technology mean that we can communicate via computers and phone wires and are able to interact with others without leaving our homes. What is built next must reflect our changing needs for privacy and community.

Connections!

BUILDINGS

Index

☆ **PICTURE CREDITS** P1 Ian Lambot/Arcaid. P3 Top: World; bottom: Comstock. P4 Top far left: World; top left: Ace; top right: Ace; right: Ace; bottom: Architecture Collection. P5 Top left: World; top middle: Ace; top right: Ace; bottom left: World; bottom right: Ace. P6 Top right: World; top left: Ace; bottom left: Camera Press; bottom right: Frank Spooner Pictures; bottom panel: Comstock. P11 Top: World; far left: Ace; middle left: Rex Features; center: World; right: Comstock; bottom: Comstock. P12 Left: Ace; right top: GSF Picture Library; right middle: GSF Picture Library; right bottom: Comstock. P13 Top left: FLPA; top right, middle left, middle right: Architectural Association; bottom left: World; bottom middle: B&C Alexander; bottom right: AC Press Services. P14 Top left: World; top right: World; middle left: World; middle center: World; middle right: World; bottom left: Architectural Association; bottom right: Arcaid. P15 Top left: World; top center: Architectural Association; top right: Architectural Association; middle left: Architectural Association; middle center: World Pictures; middle right: World; bottom left: Architectural Association; bottom center: World; bottom right: World. P16 Top: Camera Press; left: The Image Bank; right: World. P17 Left: Architectural Association; right: Rex Features. P18 Left: Architectural Association; middle: Zeta; right: Architectural Association; far right: Architectural Association. P19 AC Press Services. P20 Top: World; middle: Hutchinson Library; bottom Britstock - IFA; bottom left: Bruce Coleman; bottom right: British Antarctic Survey. P21 Top right: Katz Pictures; top center Ace; middle: Bruce Coleman; bottom: Eye Ubiquitous; panel: Comstock. P22 Left: Arcaid; right: Architectural Association; bottom: London Transport Museum. P23 Panel: Comstock; top left: Robert Francis; top center left: Architectural Association; top center right: World; top right: World; bottom left: World; bottom right: World. P25 Left: Architectural Association; center left: Architectural Association; center right: Architectural Association; right: Arcaid; bottom: Ace. P26 Top: Comstock; bottom right: Royal Geographical Society. P27 left: Bruce Coleman; right: Representation Plus UK. P28 Top left: D.S. Dorman; top right: World; middle left: Architectural Association; middle center: World; middle right: B&C Alexander; middle far right: Sims; panel: Comstock. P29 Top: Architectural Association; bottom: World; Panel: Comstock. P30 Top left: Range/Bettmann/UPI; top right: Mirror Syndication International; bottom left: Arcaid; bottom center AC Press Services; bottom center right: AC Press Services; bottom far right: Hutchison Library. P31 Top: Frank Spooner Pictures; bottom: Magnum Photos; Panel: Comstock.